Mindful SPACES

MINDFULNESS AND MY EMOTIONS

Written by Dr. Rhianna Watts and Katie Woolley
Illustrated by Sarah Jennings

For bulk sales to employers, member groups and health-related companies, contact Mayo Clinic at SpecialSalesMayoBooks@mayo.edu.

Proceeds from the sale of every book benefit important medical research and education at Mayo Clinic.

First American Edition 2024

MAYO CLINIC PRESS
200 First St. SW
Rochester, MN 55905
mcpress.mayoclinic.org

To stay informed about Mayo Clinic Press, please subscribe to our free e-newsletter at mcpress.mayoclinic.org or follow us on social media.

ISBN: 979-8-887-70135-6 (paperback) | 979-8-887-70136-3 (ebook) | 979-8-887-70118-9 (library binding)

Library of Congress Cataloging-in-Publication Data is available upon request.

MANUFACTURED IN CHINA

SAFETY PRECAUTIONS

We recommend adult supervision at all times while doing the exercises and activities in this book, particularly outdoors and activities involving exercise, glue, and scissors. When you are doing creative activities:

- Cover surfaces.
- Tie back long hair.
- Ask an adult for help with cutting.
- Check all ingredients for allergens.

Contents

BEING MINDFUL OF EMOTIONS

Emotions are the thoughts in your head and the feelings in your body that drive you to act and react to the world around you.

Mindfulness means slowing down and taking the time to pay attention to what's going on inside your body and your mind, as well as what is happening around you right now.

Mindfulness can help you understand your emotions better, so you can choose how you want to respond to the world.

Exercise

Three Breaths

In the morning, take a few moments to notice your breathing. Sit quietly, with your body straight. Relax and close your eyes.

1. Breathe air in through your nose. Notice how the air feels in your nostrils.
2. Breathe out.
3. Breathe in again and, this time, imagine the air moving down into your chest and back up again.
4. Breathe out.
5. Breathe in for a third time and feel your tummy get bigger as you take in a deep breath.
6. Breathe out.

HOW THIS EXERCISE HELPS

Mindful breathing helps you focus on what is happening right now.

THOUGHTS AND FEELINGS

When the thoughts in your head meet the sensations in your body, an emotion develops. Emotions are like the weather, constantly changing. In fact, the weather can be a good way to describe your emotions: "I feel happy, like a sunny day!"

Your daily thoughts can be a mix of creative, kind, funny, hopeful, and thankful ones. But they can also be angry, unkind, or full of worry.

The feelings in your body can be strong, too. Have you ever felt your heart beat quickly or a tightening sensation in your tummy?

What's the Weather Like?

In the morning, pay attention to your thoughts and feelings
and write a sentence describing your emotions in a notepad.
Don't forget to add the date!

MONDAY		I feel worried, like a rain cloud.
TUESDAY		I feel a little worried today.
WEDNESDAY		I feel happy, like a sunny day.
THURSDAY		I feel angry inside my tummy.
FRIDAY		I feel very disappointed today, like the rain won't go away.
SATURDAY		Today, I feel as hopeful as a rainbow.
SUNDAY		It is the end of the week and I feel all sorts of feelings, like lots of clouds of emotion.

HOW THIS ACTIVITY HELPS

Taking the time to focus inward on your thoughts and
feelings can help you better understand your emotions,
so that you are ready to begin a new day.

FOCUS IN AND LOOK OUT

It isn't always easy to tune into your emotions but
mindfulness can help you become more aware of them.

Instead of wishing your thoughts and feelings away,
or wanting to change them, you can begin to accept
them and understand how they may be useful.

Mindful Garden

Take a moment to focus your mind on this exercise.

1. Get yourself comfortable and focus on your breath. Take in three breaths and feel your body relax.
2. Imagine a garden in your mind. What does it look like? Is it bursting with flowers? Is there a pond? What animals can you see?
3. Walk around your garden and pay attention to the feel of the ground.
4. Tune into the smells and sounds you can hear.
5. If your mind wanders, try and bring it back to your garden.

HOW THIS EXERCISE HELPS

Our busy minds do like to wander! Practicing focusing your mind on one thing can help you train it to be more mindful and less restless!

DIFFERENT EMOTIONS

All emotions are useful, and there is no such thing as a 'bad' emotion. Different emotions tell you about your world and offer clues as to how you might want to respond to it in that moment.

Being mindful of your emotions and how they help you respond to the world means you can begin to welcome them as they come and go.

If you see something that looks like a snake in your yard, you might think, "Oh no, this poisonous snake will bite me!" Your body might shiver, your heart might beat faster, and your hands might feel sweaty.

These thoughts and feelings have developed into an emotion—fear—and it might make you want to run away.

Emotion Bingo!

In pairs or small groups, play a game of Emotion Bingo.

1. Create bingo boards using the emotions below.
   Choose 6 of these 8 emotions and write them in your grid.
2. Then, write out the 8 emotions on separate pieces of paper and fold them up.
3. One of you reads out the emotion on the paper, while the others cross it off their grid if they have it.
4. As each emotion is read out and crossed off, talk about times you have felt that emotion. What happened? What thoughts did you have at the time? Do you remember noticing anything in your body? How did you handle the emotion?
5. The first person to cross out all the emotions on their grid is the winner.
6. What emotion did you feel as the winner? What did you feel if you lost? How did you choose to handle your emotion?

HOW THIS ACTIVITY HELPS

This game can help you talk about different emotions with your family and friends.

WHAT SHOULD I DO?

You make many choices every day. For example, you choose what you'd like to eat for breakfast and what story you want to read at bedtime. Many choices are easy and you won't need to spend a lot of time thinking about them.

Sometimes, decisions are harder to make. As your thoughts and feelings develop into emotions, these emotions can help you with your decision-making in the present moment.

If an activity makes you feel happy, you might want to do more of it. If playing with friends makes you happy, you might ask one over to play.

If you feel angry, you might want to fight back. Understanding that you are angry, figuring out why you feel that way, and then breathing the anger out might help you make a better decision.

Exercise

Stop, Wait, Go!

Try this traffic light exercise to help you stop and think before you act.

1. **STOP:** your traffic light is red. Stop whatever you are doing, and take a slow deep breath.
2. **WAIT:** your traffic light is yellow. Pause for a moment and notice what is happening inside your body and around you. What do you think and feel? What do you want to do?
3. **GO:** your traffic light is green. Having checked in with your thoughts and feelings, decide what's the best way to respond, and go do it.

HOW THIS EXERCISE HELPS

Taking a moment to listen to your thoughts and feelings as you breathe, before choosing how to act, can help you decide what you want to do.

KNOWING MYSELF

The thoughts in your head are often full of judgement. For example, you might judge how good your drawing is and think it isn't as good as your friend's.

Sometimes judgements are useful, for example, thinking "It is not okay to hurt someone." But other times they can keep you feeling unhappy or stressed: "My drawings are always terrible."

Mindfulness can help you become more aware of these judgements, and learn to let them go by refocusing your mind on other non-judgemental thoughts. For example, "Sometimes my drawings look like what I want them to, sometimes they don't. I can keep practicing."

Understanding your thoughts and feelings without judging them can also help you feel more confident in yourself. It means you can begin to trust yourself to either act on an emotion or let it pass, building your self-esteem and your confidence.

Wise Owl

Owls are believed to be wise creatures who trust their thoughts, feelings, and actions. You can be a wise owl, too.

1. Write down some positive phrases on pieces of paper.
2. Fold them up and put them in a jar.
3. You could decorate your jar with natural objects, such as twigs, leaves, and feathers, to make it look like an owl.
4. Every morning, choose a piece of paper and read the advice from your wise old owl to give you confidence.

Activity

MY LIFE IS MOVING FORWARD.

I AM STRONG.

I LOVE ME.

I AM ENOUGH.

TODAY, I FEEL CONFIDENT IN MY ABILITIES.

I AM EXACTLY WHERE I NEED TO BE.

HOW THIS ACTIVITY HELPS

Repeating positive statements regularly challenges the unhelpful, and sometimes judgemental, thoughts in your head.

MOMENTS OF HAPPINESS

Happiness is your body's way of telling you something is right and that you are well.

What do you notice in your body and mind when you feel happy? Do you feel warm, comfortable, and content, or do you feel light, springy, and energized? Is your mind full of positive thoughts?

Paying attention to your emotions can help you notice pleasant experiences, allowing you to soak up more of each positive moment. You can choose, in the moment, to do more of the activities that bring you happiness.

My Happiness Box

1. Find an old cardboard box, for example an old shoebox.

2. Decorate your box with pictures, photos, colors, and words that mean 'happiness' to you.

3. Fill your box with reminders of 'happiness.' This could be photos of family trips where you had fun, your favorite song or toy, a piece of schoolwork you are proud of, or anything that makes you feel happy.

4. Every day, try to stop and notice times you feel happy. Notice where you are, what you are thinking, feeling, and doing. If you can, collect something to put in your box to remind you of this moment. For example, collecting a leaf or flower might remind you of how happy you felt outdoors today.

HOW THIS ACTIVITY HELPS

Pausing, noticing, and collecting moments of happiness can help you soak up positive experiences as they happen, learn what is important to you to feel happy, and build more positive experiences into your life.

CLOUDS OF ANGER

We all get angry sometimes. Anger is your body's way of telling you that something is happening that you do not like or want. Anger can be helpful as it tells us when something is wrong and needs to change.

Can you think of a time when you have felt angry? How did you feel in your body? Did your muscles stiffen up? Did your breathing change? What thoughts went through your mind? What did your thoughts and feelings make you want to do?

Ahh!

I don't like losing.

I hate you!

It's not fair!

Paint It Out

Paint a picture of your anger on a piece of paper. What colors will you use? Perhaps your anger looks like straight red lines or maybe it is a jumble of wiggly rainbow colors? It might even be a picture of dark rain clouds over a stormy sea.

How This ACTIVITY Helps

Painting helps you focus on how an emotion makes you think and feel. Once you understand your thoughts and feelings, you can work out how you want to respond.

ANGRY ACTIONS

Feeling angry is okay and can be helpful. If you can learn to listen to your mind and body to work out why you are angry, it can help you know what you want to do about it.

You might get angry when you lose a board game or when someone says something unkind to you. You might want to lash out at what has made you feel upset.

If you are angry about losing a board game because you like to be good at things, you might want to try and accept that you cannot be the best all the time. It's kind to be happy that someone else has won.

20

If you are angry because someone has said something unkind to you, you might want to talk to a trusted adult about this. It's never okay for someone to be unkind and it would make sense that you feel angry.

Exercise

Breathe It Out

1. Next time you feel angry, pause and notice where you feel the anger in your body.

2. Take a deep breath and imagine that breath filling that part of your body.

3. Breathe into the angry feelings and then breathe them out.

HOW THIS EXERCISE HELPS

Pausing and breathing gives time for some of the heat of the angry feelings to go away. This helps you find the time to listen to their important message and work out how you want to respond, without being overwhelmed by them.

WAVES OF WORRY

We all feel worried at times. When you are worried, your body might feel uncomfortable and your mind might become full of thoughts, as you imagine that 'bad' things are going to happen.

Worry is your body's way of telling you that something scary or upsetting may happen in the future, which you might need to get ready for.

Have you ever felt worried?
What thoughts were in your head?
How did your body feel?
Did your face feel hot?
Was your mind racing?
Did you have butterflies in your tummy and a dry mouth?

Strong Mountain

It can be hard to quiet down worried thoughts and feelings. Slowing down and noticing what you are thinking and feeling can help you understand why you are feeling worried and decide what you want to do about it.

3. Pay attention to your thoughts and any worries you have as your arms go up. Imagine they are clouds swirling around the mountain.

2. Breathe in and slowly raise your arms high above your head, like a strong mountain.

4. As you breathe out and lower your arms, imagine those clouds blowing away.

1. Stand with your feet apart and your arms by your sides.

HOW THIS EXERCISE HELPS

When we worry, we are often caught up in our thoughts. We feel trapped. Pausing, breathing, and standing strong like a mountain, can help anchor us to the present moment, so that we can feel calmer.

WORRYING THOUGHTS

You might feel worried about a piece of homework
or perhaps you are worried about a family member.
Taking the time to notice your worrying thoughts
can help you deal with this emotion.

If you are worried about school,
you might decide to talk
to your teacher and see
if they can give you
tips on how to complete
your homework.

If you are worried about a
family member, you could talk to a
trusted adult. You could even write down your
worries in a diary. We all worry from time to
time, so it makes sense that you will, too.

Mindfulness can help you find ways to listen to your
worries, discover why they are there, and help you
decide how you want to respond to them.

The Worry Jar

This activity can help you pay attention to your worries.

Activity

1. Ask an adult to find you an old, clean jelly jar with a lid.

2. Decorate the jar however you wish.

3. Write down any worries when they come to you. *"I sometimes worry about..."*

4. Put your worry in the jar and shut the lid tight.

HOW THIS ACTIVITY HELPS

A worry jar can help you pay attention to your thoughts and feelings. Taking the time to notice them will help you decide which ones you want to let go and which ones you want to return to and do something about.

SIGNS OF SADNESS

There are lots of things that can make you feel sad;
some might be big and some might be small.
Sadness is your body's way of telling you that you
are missing something that is important to you.

You might feel sad for
a little while when your
favorite toy is broken
or if your friends
are playing a game
without you.

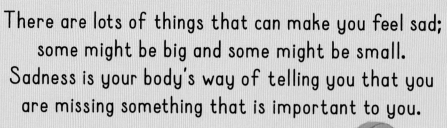

Sometimes, your sad feeling will take
longer to go away, and that's okay,
too. If your pet dies, it will take time to
feel happy again. Slowly, you will find
yourself noticing happy moments, even
though you might still feel sad at times.

Activity

Sadness Calls

Sometimes changes in our lives can make us feel sad.

1. Look around you and spot one thing that has changed that makes you feel a little sad. It might be a flower that has died, or maybe the sun is no longer shining.
2. Write a poem about your sadness and how this change makes you feel.
3. Then look around for a change that brings you happiness.
4. Draw a picture of what makes you happy. You could keep it by your bed.

Talking to a friend or a trusted grown-up can help. You might like to write down your feelings in a diary. Mindfulness can help you find ways to do things that make YOU feel better, too, such as going on a long walk.

HOW THIS ACTIVITY HELPS

Taking the time to listen to your thoughts and feelings as you write about them and draw them can help you understand them better.

FIND THE QUIET

Your busy thoughts and feelings can make it hard to relax. Your emotions can, at times, feel overwhelming. So, when your body wants to rest, your emotions can make it difficult for your mind to switch off.

A mindful activity can help you begin to feel more relaxed.

Activity

My Glitter Globe

1. Find a small plastic bottle and add some glitter, so the bottle is half full. Then, ask an adult to help you fill the bottle with water right to the top.

2. Put the lid on your bottle and close it tightly. Shake it up to mix all of the ingredients.

3. The glitter in your globe will swirl when you shake it, but settle slowly when you stop.

4. When you need a moment of calm, such as before you go to sleep, sit with your glitter globe and take a slow, deep breath in and out. Shake your globe, noticing the glitter swirl, like your thoughts and feelings do at the end of a busy day.

5. Stop shaking the bottle and watch the glitter settle, letting your thoughts and feelings settle, too.

6. Breathe slowly in and out. Notice your mind and body settling with the glitter with each breath in and out.

HOW THIS ACTIVITY HELPS

The glitter globe is like your mind and body. It can be full of busy thoughts and feelings swirling around. Pausing, noticing this, and giving your mind and body time to settle can help you find the quiet.

29

MINDFULNESS TIPS

Mindfulness helps anchor you in the present moment. It helps you feel confident and ready to tackle the day. It can also help you navigate big emotions and it can help you find moments of calm in your busy world.

Here are some tips to help you practice mindfulness.

* You can practice mindfulness anywhere and at any time. Mindfulness simply means choosing to pay attention to what is happening inside your mind and body, and what is happening around you, in the present moment, right here and right now.

* You can do this by sitting and focusing on your breath for five minutes in bed before you go to sleep, or you could do this by focusing on what you can see and hear while walking to school!

* Your breath and how it feels in your body is very important. Paying attention to your breath helps you focus on what is happening in the present moment. Your breath is like an anchor for your mind and body. It can stop them from floating away.

* It's okay if you start to feel a little bored or if your mind wanders. If you can, just notice this and refocus your mind where you want it to be. If you get stuck, be kind to yourself. Remember, you are learning a new skill and you can always try again another day.

* If your body starts to feel uncomfortable, notice where in your body you feel any aches and move into a more comfortable position. However, always stop doing an exercise if you feel pain.

INDEX